Happiness

summersdale

HAPPINESS

Summersdale Publishers Ltd
46 West Street
Chichester
West Sussex
PO19 1RP
UK

www.summersdale.com

Printed and bound in China

ISBN: 978-1-84953-032-3

Substantial discounts on bulk quantities of Summersdale books are available to corporations, professional associations and other organisations. For details contact Summersdale Publishers by telephone: +44 (0) 1243771107, fax: +44 (0) 1243 786300 or email: nicky@summersdale.com.

Happiness

thoughts & quotations
for every day

Happiness is when what you think, what you say and what you do are in harmony.

Mahatma Gandhi

*One joy scatters a
hundred griefs.*

Chinese proverb

Every time you smile at someone, it is an action of love, a gift to that person, a beautiful thing.

Mother Teresa

He who sows courtesy reaps friendship,
and he who plants kindness gathers love.

St Basil of Caesarea

Happiness is not something ready made. It comes from your own actions.

Dalai Lama

Have patience and endure: this unhappiness will one day be beneficial.

Ovid

Happiness is not an ideal of reason, but of imagination.

Immanuel Kant

*Mindfulness helps us to regain the paradise
we thought we had lost.*

Thich Nhat Hanh

I think I began learning long ago that those who are happiest are those who do the most for others.

Booker T. Washington

Happiness consists not in having much,
but in being content with little.

Marguerite Gardiner

Happiness is the key to success.

Albert Schweitzer

If you want to be happy, be.

Leo Tolstoy

Independence is happiness.

Susan B. Anthony

*The righteous man is happy in this world,
and he is happy in the next.*

The Dhammapada

*Turn your face to the sun and the shadows
fall behind you.*

Maori proverb

Humour is the great thing, the saving thing.

Mark Twain

Those who make many friends… make society a better place and lead happy, satisfying lives.

Daisaku Ikeda

Our life is what our thoughts make it.

Marcus Aurelius

He who knows that enough is enough will always have enough.

Lao Tzu

You will never be happier than you expect.
To change your happiness, change
your expectation.

Bette Davis

The most wasted of all days is that on which one has not laughed.

Nicolas Chamfort

A great obstacle to happiness is to expect too much happiness.

Bernard de Fontenelle

Weeping may endure for a night, but joy cometh in the morning.

Psalms 30:5

Let no one ever come to you without leaving better and happier.

Mother Teresa

Most folks are about as happy as they make up their minds to be.

Abraham Lincoln

Happiness never decreases by being shared.

Buddha

The best way to secure future happiness is to be as happy as is rightfully possible today.

Charles W. Eliot

There are two ways of spreading light: to be the candle or the mirror that reflects it.

Edith Wharton

Happiness… lies in the joy of achievement, in the thrill of creative effort.

Franklin D. Roosevelt

The grand essentials of happiness are: something to do, something to love and something to hope for.

Alexander Chalmers

The more we are aware of to be grateful for, the happier we become.

Ezra Taft Benson

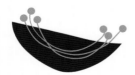

Happiness is not a goal; it is a by-product.

Eleanor Roosevelt

Happiness is a habit — cultivate it.

Elbert Hubbard

But the man worthwhile is the one who will smile when everything goes dead wrong.

Ella Wheeler Wilcox

*Every lot has enough happiness
provided for it.*

Fyodor Dostoevsky

Those who bring sunshine into the lives of others cannot keep it from themselves.

J. M. Barrie

We act as though comfort and luxury were the chief requirements of life, when all that we need to make us really happy is something to be enthusiastic about.

Charles Kingsley

So long as we can lose any happiness,
we possess some.

Booth Tarkington

Happiness is like a butterfly which, when pursued, is always beyond our grasp, but, if you will sit down quietly, may alight upon you.

Nathaniel Hawthorne

A happy life consists not in the absence,
but in the mastery of hardships.

Helen Keller

All the statistics in the world can't measure the warmth of a smile.

Chris Hart

If you ever find happiness by hunting for it, you will find it, as the old woman did her lost spectacles, safe on her own nose all the time.

Josh Billings

Always laugh when you can. It is cheap medicine.

Lord Byron

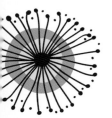

*There is no cosmetic for beauty
like happiness.*

Marguerite Gardiner

Illusory joy is often worth more than genuine sorrow.

René Descartes

Mix a little foolishness with your serious plans. It is lovely to be silly at the right moment.

Horace

For every minute you are angry you lose sixty seconds of happiness.

Ralph Waldo Emerson

To be kind to all, to like many and love a few, to be needed and wanted by those we love, is certainly the nearest we can come to happiness.

Mary Stuart

Gladness of heart is the life of man and the joyfulness of man is length of days.

Ecclesiastes

The robbed that smiles, steals something from the thief.

William Shakespeare, *Othello*

He who enjoys doing and enjoys what he has done is happy.

Johann Wolfgang von Goethe

Happiness arises in a state of peace, not of tumult.

Ann Radcliffe

Grief can take care of itself, but to get the full value of a joy you must have somebody to divide it with.

Mark Twain

Content makes poor men rich; discontent makes rich men poor.

Benjamin Franklin

If I keep a green bough in my heart the singing bird will come.

Chinese proverb

If only we'd stop trying to be happy we could have a pretty good time.

Edith Wharton

A happy life consists in tranquillity of mind.

Marcus Tullius Cicero

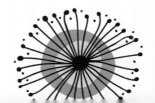

A kind heart is a fountain of gladness, making everything in its vicinity freshen into smiles.

Washington Irving

Forget not that the earth delights to feel your bare feet and the winds long to play with your hair.

Kahlil Gibran

Think of all the beauty still left around
you and be happy.

Anne Frank

Happiness often sneaks in through a door
you didn't know you left open.

John Barrymore

You're the blacksmith of your own happiness.

Norwegian proverb

Be glad of life because it gives you the chance to love, to work, to play and to look up at the stars.

Henry van Dyke

Happiness cannot come from without. It must come from within.

Helen Keller

It is not how much we have, but how much we enjoy, that makes happiness.

Charles Spurgeon

Joy is the will which labours, which overcomes obstacles, which knows triumph.

William Butler Yeats

Be happy. It's one way of being wise.

Colette

But what is happiness except the simple harmony between a man and the life he leads?

Albert Camus

Talk happiness. The world is sad enough without your woe. No path is wholly rough.

Ella Wheeler Wilcox

Pleasure in the task puts perfection in the work.

Aristotle

Action may not always bring happiness,
but there is no happiness without action.

Benjamin Disraeli

Every day, tell at least one person something you like, admire or appreciate about them.

Richard Carlson

Happiness belongs to the self-sufficient.

Aristotle

Greater happiness comes with simplicity than with complexity.

Buddha

If you want others to be happy, practise compassion. If you want to be happy, practise compassion.

Dalai Lama

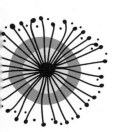

Let us be of good cheer, remembering that the misfortunes hardest to bear are those which never happen.

James Russell Lowell

One must never look for happiness: one meets it by the way.

Isabelle Eberhardt

To render ourselves happy is to love our work and find in it our pleasure.

Françoise Bertaut de Motteville

There is no duty which we so much underrate as the duty of being happy.

Robert Louis Stevenson

*There is only one happiness in life, to
love and be loved.*

George Sand

A handful of happiness is better than a load full of wisdom.

Russian proverb

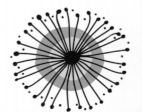

*Pleasure disappoints:
possibility never.*

Søren Kierkegaard

Happiness is the meaning and the purpose of life, the whole aim and end of human existence.

Aristotle

There are those who give with joy, and that joy is their reward.

Kahlil Gibran

Against the assault of laughter
nothing can stand.

Mark Twain

All animals, except man, know that the principal business of life is to enjoy it.

Samuel Butler

Laughter is the sensation of feeling good all over and showing it principally in one place.

Josh Billings

Wisdom is the supreme part of happiness.

Sophocles

True happiness... is not attained through self-gratification, but through fidelity to a worthy purpose.

Helen Keller

Happiness is a perfume you cannot pour on others without getting a few drops on yourself.

Ralph Waldo Emerson

Have you enjoyed this book? If so, why not write a review
on your favourite website?

Thanks very much for buying this
Summersdale book.

www.summersdale.com

Songs I like —

- Stevie Wonder — you R so beau
- UB40 — the one u used to sing
- That Xmas song by the guy with
  the rotten teeth + girl — NY —
- Anything by Al green
- Elton John
= Ennio Morricone composer
- Brahms — How lovely is thy dw
- YoYo Ma Plays Ennio Mor